short

u

Words & Letters 5

KNOWLEDGE BOOKS

mud	bug
bus	sun
run	mug
jug	

u

mud

bug

5

bus

7

sun

8

9

run

mug

13

jug

14

15

mud	bug
bus	sun
run	mug
jug	

Knowledge Books and Software
PO Box 50 Sandgate, Queensland 4017 Australia
p. +617-55680288 f. +617-55680277 email: sales@kbs.com.au

First Published 2022
ISBN 9781922516770
Text and editing: Carole Crimeen
Design and layout: Suzanne Fletcher
Publisher: Robert Watts

Series Information: **Sounds and Letters**

Credits
Photographs: Cover © NadyaEugene; p. 1 © Luis Louro, Andrey Arkusha, Zurbagan, vlavetal; p. 3 © Pixabay; p. 5 © Alik Mulikov; p. 7 © Supertrooper; p. 9 © Iakov Kalinin; p. 11 © Monkey Business Images; p. 13 © Natasha Gusarova; p. 15 © Nils Versemann/Shutterstock.

Phonic support books are a wonderful resource for emergent readers as they encourage independent reading and help students make the link between letters and the sounds they represent.

Have students identify the images on the title page to listen for the long or short vowel sound that they will hear through the book.

Encourage students to point to each word as they read through the book.

ISBN: 9781922516770

9 781922 516770 >

KNOWLEDGE BOOKS

Sounds&
Letters